CRYPTOCURRENCY WORLD

© Copyright 2017 - All rights reserved.

The contents of this book may not be reproduced, duplicated or transmitted without direct written permission from the author. Under no circumstances will any legal responsibility or blame be held against the publisher for any reparation, damages, or monetary loss due to the information herein, either directly or indirectly.

Legal Notice:
You cannot amend, distribute, sell, use, quote or paraphrase any part or the content within this book without the consent of the author.
Charlie Pryce

Disclaimer Notice:
Please note the information contained within this document is for educational and entertainment purposes only. No warranties of any kind are expressed or implied. Readers acknowledge that the author is not engaging in the rendering of legal, financial, medical or professional advice. Please consult a licensed professional before attempting any techniques outlined in this book.
By reading this document, the reader agrees that under no circumstances are is the author responsible for any losses, direct or indirect, which are incurred as a result of the use of information contained within this document, including, but not limited to, —errors, omissions, or inaccuracies.

CRYPTOCURRENCY WORLD

BEGINNER'S GUIDE TO SOME OF THE TOP CRYPTOCURRENCIES: BITCOIN, ETHEREUM, LITECOIN +

Charlie Pryce

https://www.amazon.com/dp/B077PG7BBX

Table of Contents

Introduction	1
Chapter One: What Are Cryptocurrencies?	3
Chapter Two: What is a Blockchain	11
Chapter Three: Exchanges and Wallets	15
Chapter Four: Bitcoin and Other Cryptocurrencies	21
Chapter Five: Cryptocurrency Regulations	27
Chapter Six: Your Mindset	33
Conclusion	35

INTRODUCTION

I want to thank you for taking the time to read my guide. Cryptocurrency is a hot topic right now, especially given the bull run of the market this year. Prices have shot up, reaching dizzy heights never before seen and never even thought of with digital currencies. And, although things have settled back down again now, there is nothing to say that the prices won't rise again, as interest in cryptocurrency continues to rise.

Not everyone is au fait with cryptocurrencies though. Not everyone knows what they are, what the blockchain is and how it works. Not everyone is aware of what a Bitcoin is and how that works, so that's what my guide is all about. It's for the newbies, for those who don't really know what the word of cryptocurrency is all about and wouldn't know where to start if they wanted to jump into the market.

I am not going into great technical detail here; you will get an overview of what the cryptocurrencies are, what a blockchain is and then a look at some of the most popular and upcoming cryptocurrencies in the market right now. It is a starting point for you; a point from which you can decide whether you want to invest any time or money in the hottest market prospect in existence.

Chapter One:
What Are Cryptocurrencies?

The very first cryptocurrency came about after a white paper was released in 2008. This paper came from an unknown person/group of persons called Satoshi Nakamoto, and it detailed a digital currency called Bitcoin. This digital currency was about to revolutionize the world of money and change the way we use it forever.

Why would someone come up with this idea? I mean, we already have money that we can spend, transfer to others or exchange for other currencies. The reason behind the Bitcoin was clear – it's a currency that can be spent fast, anywhere in the world, without any restrictions and with no borders. And there is no devaluation of the main cryptocurrencies like there is with paper money or fiat currency, as it is known.

Even before the Bitcoin was created, the idea of cryptocurrency existed. Does that surprise you? There were several attempts made at introducing a system of digital currency. Before learning more about Bitcoins and other cryptos, it is important to understand the history of cryptocurrencies. There were several attempts made at the creation of a system of digital currency, but the former versions were centralized, unlike the versions that exist today.

A really interesting aspect of cryptocurrencies is that they weren't intended to be invented in the manner in which they are known today. For instance, the aim of Nakamoto when he published the white paper on cryptocurrencies was the creation of a peer-to-peer electronic cash system and nothing else. Several attempts had been made in the past to create a system of digital cash, but they always failed due to the troubles with centralization. Satoshi was aware that the idea of creating another online cash system that is centralized would just spell failure. So, instead, he decided to create a digitized cash system that is decentralized, and this led to the creation of Bitcoins. Bitcoin was the first cryptocurrency that was fully decentralized and had no central authority governing it. Bitcoin was created to be the property of the entire community of users and no one else.

Back when Bitcoin was created, the value of a single token was a little more than the value of a cent. However, the value of this cryptocurrency grew rather quickly and, by the end of 2009, a single token was valued around $27. With the tremendous increase in its popularity, the value of a single Bitcoin was around $7500 in the year 2017. Going back to the creation of Bitcoin, a major problem that Nakamoto was facing was to prevent double spending. Double spending refers to the act where the owner is spending the same money twice. The control over the spending and also the number of cryptos present in the digitized space was controlled by a central authority in the past, and therefore, all the previous attempts made at the creation of a digitized currency were centralized. This was done to keep a check on double spending. Nakamoto figured out an ingenious manner in which double spending could be curbed without the need for a central authority. In a

What Are Cryptocurrencies?

decentralized system of digital currency, every user needs to agree on every account balance for the transaction to work. However, Nakamoto managed to create a system of digital currencies that are free of all intermediaries. Complete consensus is necessary to ensure the validity of a transaction and the entire system will crumble if there is any disagreement. All this might seem quite complicated, but the creation of Bitcoins put an end to all this.

With fiat currency, the Federal Reserve, central banks, and the governments control the value, manipulating it to suit themselves. They frequently "print" more money, pushing it into the economy knowing they will get it back in interest payments and the more there is of currency, the less value it has. With the cryptocurrency, it is different.

All transactions involving conventional forms of currency, excluding all pure cash transfers involve third parties or other intermediaries like banks. All the intermediaries charge certain fees for executing these transactions. Not just that, there is a lot of risks involved in such transactions as well. For instance, when you receive a check from someone, what is the guarantee that there are sufficient funds in the issuer's account? This is where cryptocurrencies differ from regular currencies.

For a start, it's decentralized. This means there is no central bank, no government, and no intermediary at all involved in it. Cryptocurrencies don't involve any intermediaries. Every transaction is made directly between two parties, making them much faster and much cheaper, as well as eliminating the risk of someone else interfering in your transactions and charging you for the privilege of it. All transactions are executed between the transacting parties directly and are confirmed instantaneously.

With fiat currencies, there is the problem of hyperinflation. Cryptocurrencies solve this problem by placing the control of money supply in the software used instead of the government. The software or the protocol has been designed in such a manner that the total supply of the currency is fixed. Regardless of an increase in the demand for a particular cryptocurrency, the supply will not increase.

And second, unlike the fiat currency, there is a hard limit on many cryptocurrencies of how much of it will be released. The Bitcoin, for example, is limited to 21 million coins and the last of these is expected to be mined in around 2040. After that, there will be no more, and supply and demand will ensure the value is retained.

Let's remove the technicalities. A simple definition of a cryptocurrency is that it is no more than entries in a database that cannot be changed without a set of specific conditions being fulfilled. And, really, this is how any money is defined. The money that sits in your bank account, for example, is nothing more than an entry on a database and, for it to be changed, it must fulfill specific conditions. All money is found in a database as a verified entry, and that database contains accounts, transactions, and balances. The only real difference here is that the currency is not physical and there is no intermediary controlling it – the only person that controls it is you.

So, how do these cryptocurrencies work? We'll use the Bitcoin as an example here. Bitcoin is made up of a network of peers. These peers are computers or nodes on the network, and each one retains a complete history of all transactions and account balances. This history is called the blockchain, and we'll discuss that in the next chapter.

A transaction is nothing more than a file that says, "A gives x amount of Bitcoin to B." That transaction is signed by something called a private key, an encrypted password if you like that confirms the identity of the payee. Once the transaction has been signed, it is sent to the entire network, to every peer on that network (and there are millions). For the transaction to complete it must be confirmed, and this is a critical point in cryptocurrency. Confirmation of a transaction is done by a miner, and these are the people that verify each transaction as legitimate and transfer them across the network. Once this is done, each node on the network must add it to their database, and it becomes a part of the blockchain and cannot be reversed.

So, a cryptocurrency is nothing more than an entry in a decentralized consensus- database. They are built on strong cryptography, and they are not secured by any one person; instead, they are secured by a mathematical algorithm. To understand the cryptocurrency properties, we must separate the transactional from the monetary properties.

Transactional:

Cryptocurrency transactions are:
- **Irreversible.** Once confirmed, a transaction cannot be reversed in any way.

- **Pseudonymous.** Accounts and transactions are not connected to any real-world identity. Everything is done using a cryptocurrency address, which is a random string of characters that cannot be connected to your real identity. Multiple addresses can be created without ever giving out any sensitive or private information.

- **Global and fast.** Transactions are almost instant, confirmed within minutes, and because the nodes are global, this is irrespective of your physical location. You can send a transaction to anywhere in the world or to your next-door neighbor in the same amount of time.

- **Secure.** All funds are locked up in a cryptographic system. Only the person who has the private cryptography key can make a transaction from that account, and this is an unbreakable scheme, stronger than Fort Knox!

- **Permissionless.** You don't need to ask permission from anyone to use cryptocurrency; it is nothing more than software that, once downloaded, enables you to send and receive cryptocurrency with no one to stop you or interfere.

Monetary:

- **Controlled Supply.** Pretty much all cryptocurrencies have a limited supply, and this is written into the code at the start along with a supply schedule, meaning the supply of any cryptocurrency can be calculated at any given moment. Controlled supply helps to increase the value of the cryptocurrencies.

- **No Debt**. Any fiat currency is created through debt, and any number you see on your account represents that debt, nothing more than an IOU system. Cryptocurrencies represent only themselves

To truly understand just how revolutionary the cryptocurrency is, you must take both types of property into account. An irreversible, permissionless and pseudonymous payment method is nothing more than an attack on the way governments and central banks control the money. They remove the scope that these financial and governing institutions have over monetary policy, and they remove the control that the central banks have on inflation and deflation through manipulation of supply.

CHAPTER TWO:
WHAT IS A BLOCKCHAIN

Don and Alex Tapscott, authors of "The Blockchain Revolution" describe the blockchain as "an incorruptible digital ledger of economic transactions that can be programmed to record not just financial transactions but virtually everything of value."

To understand the blockchain, imagine a spreadsheet. This spreadsheet has been duplicated millions of times over a vast computer network. Each computer on this network has been designed in such a way that it updates this spreadsheet, so each is identical. That is the blockchain.

The blockchain is a database on which all information is shared and is reconciled continually. There are some very obvious benefits to using the network in this way in that the database does not get stored in a single central location; instead, a copy is stored on every node in the network means that all records are public and are verifiable.

- Durable and Robust

Blockchain technology can be likened to the Internet in that it has robustness built in. Through the act of storing data blocks that are identical across every node, a blockchain may not be controlled by any one entity, and it has no SPOF – single point of failure.

- Incorruptible and Transparent

The blockchain network exists in what we call a "state of consensus." By this, we mean that it checks itself every 10 minutes automatically, a self-auditing system. The network will reconcile each transaction that takes place in a ten-minute period, and we call these transaction groups, 'blocks,' and there are two things that come out of this:

Incorruptibility – nothing can be altered because, to do so would require overriding the whole network, and that would take an enormous amount of computing power at a cost far more than would be gained and the value of the currency would be destroyed.

Transparency – the data is embedded as a whole on the network, which means it is public – if anything were to happen, everyone would see it.

- Network of Nodes

A network of computers or nodes makes up the blockchain, each using a piece of software that validates and relays each transaction. Each computer has a copy of the blockchain, and together they make up what we call a second level network. Each computer is a blockchain administrator and is voluntary; this is what makes the network decentralized. Each does this to be in with a chance to win currency by solving mathematical algorithms, known as mining.

- Decentralization

So, we know that the blockchain is decentralized and anything that is done n it happens on every computer on the network. There are some very important implications from this – with a new way of verifying transactions, we could find that some of the more traditional aspects of commerce transactions. And some other ways of record keeping could become public, such as land registry records and voting.

Blockchain Uses

Right now, the finance industry has the best possible use case for the blockchain technology. Take international money transfers – according to the World Bank, over $430 billion worth of transfers were sent in 2015 alone. The blockchain will remove the intermediary in these transfers, giving people the option to make direct transfers within minutes – no more fees, no more waiting for transactions to be verified by a central institution. Online transactions are also very closely connected with identity verification processes and, in years to come, we may see this expand to more kinds of identity management.

Enhanced Security

Because data is stored across the entire network, the risks of centrally held data are eliminated. There are no central points that are vulnerable to attack by a hacker. We all know the inherent problems of security on the Internet these days simply because we all rely on the use of usernames and passwords for identity protection. The blockchain throws that away and uses encryption technology instead.

We mentioned public and private keys earlier, and that is the basis for the encryption technology. The public key is a string of random characters, and this is the address of the user on the blockchain. Any transaction is recorded to the relevant public address. The private key is your password, and it is what gives you access to your cryptocurrencies, stored in a wallet. A wallet can be online or offline and is a piece of software that lets you store your assets and send or receive them. Provided you do not lose your private key or forget what it is, your assets are safe and cannot be corrupted. One safe way of retaining your password is to print it out, and this is called a paper wallet.

That is all you need to know about the blockchain right now so let's have a quick look at exchange and wallets, two very important facets to trading in cryptocurrencies.

CHAPTER THREE: EXCHANGES AND WALLETS

Wallets and exchanges are very important subjects in the cryptocurrency world so let's start with exchanges.

Exchanges

An exchange is a website where cryptocurrencies can be bought, sold and exchanged for another cryptocurrency or for fiat currencies. These are the safest places for beginners to the cryptocurrency markets and setting up an account is generally very easy. You will be required to verify your identity and your payment method. There are different types of exchanges to look out for:

- **A Trading Platform** – websites that connect buyers with sellers and charge a small fee for each transaction made

- **Direct Trading** – a platform that offers person-to-person trading, allowing people from different countries to exchange currency. There is no fixed market price; instead, the exchange rate is set by the seller.

- **Brokers** – websites that anyone can visit to purchase their cryptocurrencies. The price is set by the broker and will differ from platform to platform. These can be seen as being similar to a foreign exchange broker.

Before You Join an Exchange

Before you jump in, it is essential that you do some research so check out these things before you join an exchange:

- **Reputation**s – check through reviews, both from individuals and industries, on the exchange and visit popular forums to ask questions about any particular exchange to find out whether they are reputable or not.

- **Fees** – all exchanges should publish information about their fee structure on their website. Make sure you understand the information before you join an exchange

- **Payment Methods** – find out which methods of payment the exchange accepts. Some will accept a wide range while others will be limited, and these may not be the most convenient. Do remember that using a credit card will attract a higher fee and will require identity verification. Wire transfers take longer as they need to go to the bank; PayPal is rarely an option, so the best is often debit card.

- **Verification** – most exchanges are required by law to verify your identity before any deposit or withdrawal can happen. This can take a couple of days to complete, but it does protect you and the exchange you are using for fraud and money laundering.

- **Geo-Restrictions** – check each exchange for the countries that are supported. Some will limit trading tools to specific countries, and yours may not be one of them.

- **The rate of Exchange** – each exchange will have its own exchange rates and shop around for the best rates can save you a significant amount of money.

Wallets

Cryptocurrency wallets are pieces of software that store your public and private keys, and that interact with blockchains to let you send cryptocurrency and receive it as well as keeping an eye on your balance. You will need one of these if you want to trade in any cryptocurrency.

While wallets are used by millions of people worldwide, not everyone understands how they work. A digital wallet does not actually store currency, only the public, and the private keys. They are the interface that you use to keep an eye on your asset balance, send and receive money and carry out other transactions. When you receive a cryptocurrency from another person, they are transferring ownership of their currency to your wallet and, for you to be able to access and spend them, your private key must match the public address that the currency is stored in. If the two keys match, your digital asset balance will increase. No physical money is transferred, only a transaction record which is stored on the blockchain. There are several types of wallet to consider:

Types of Cryptocurrency Wallet

There are three main categories of wallet – hardware, software, and paper. The software wallet is broken down into three further categories – mobile, desktop or online.

- **Desktop** – downloaded onto a laptop/PC and can only be accessed from the computer they are installed on. Highest security level offered unless your computer is hacked or attacked by a virus; in this case, you risk the loss of your assets

- **Online** – on the cloud and can be accessed from all devices in all locations. Convenient but your keys are stored online, and they are controlled by an intermediary, making them vulnerable to attack and theft.

- **Mobile** – an app on your tablet or smartphone, which can be used anywhere, even in some retail stores. Small, simple and easy to use

- **Hardware** – hardware devices like USB flash drives are used to store your private keys. This is stored offline so are less vulnerable to attack and can support multiple currencies and web interfaces. Transactions are done by connecting the device to your PC, inputting a pin number and carrying out the transaction.

- **Paper** - ease of use and the highest level of security. This is a printout of your private key and must be stored safely. Using them to transfer funds is easy – transfer from a software wallet to the public address that you see on your paper wallet. And to spend, simply transfer from that address to your software wallet.

How secure are they?

Cryptocurrency wallets are secure, but the level of security will depend on which one you use and your own service provider. It is riskier to store your wallet on a web server than it is to store it offline, for example, because the online wallets are open to attack by hackers. An offline wallet cannot be hacked because it is not connected to the server and has no reliance on any third-party for security.

No matter which type of wallet you use, there are certain security precautions that you need to take. Keep in mind that, regardless of which you use, if you lose your private key, you will lose your assets. In the same way, if you get duped into sending money to a scammer, there isn't any way to get it back, and you can't reverse a transaction.

- **Back Your Wallet Up** – keep only small amounts of currency in your online wallet for daily use and keep the rest in a higher security wallet. Use cold or offline storage options, such as USB flash or paper wallet so that you can recover your wallet in the event of a loss or theft. This will NOT protect you from hackers. Back your wallet up in several different places as well

- **Keep Your Software Updated** – this will ensure that you always have the very latest in security fixes. This applies to your wallet and to your computer or mobile

- **Add Extra Security** – the more, the better, to be honest. Use long passwords that are complex and add a password for any withdrawal. Use only those wallets with good reputations and use two-factor authentication where offered. If you can, choose a wallet that has the option of multisig, requiring more than one signature for each transaction

That just about covers all you need to know about exchanges and wallets, so it's time to look at some of the more popular cryptocurrencies available.

CHAPTER FOUR:
BITCOIN AND OTHER CRYPTOCURRENCIES

There are more than 1000 cryptocurrencies in existence today, but many of them are worthless. We are going to look closely at some of the more popular ones.

Bitcoin

Usually referred to by the acronym BTC, Bitcoin was the first ever cryptocurrency to be released and remains the most popular today. It was released in 2009 by Satoshi Nakamoto and is the gold standard by which all cryptocurrencies are judged; BTC is also the most global means of digital payments. Within 8 years, Bitcoin has jumped from being worth nothing to attracting prices of more than $6000 although the sheer volatility of the digital currency market means that this price could just as easily crash back down. Bitcoin supply is set at a hard limit of 21 million coins, and over two-thirds of those have already been mined. This hard limit is what will ensure that the Bitcoin cannot be devalued. It is worth remembering that Bitcoin was the first to introduce the blockchain technology and every coin or token that follows has Bitcoin to thank for that.

The average time it takes for each Bitcoin block to be mined is around 10 minutes and, right now, the miner who wins receives a reward of 12.5 Bitcoins. It started life as 50 Bitcoins, but it is written into the code that, for every 210,000 blocks that are mined, the reward will be cut in half. The next cut down to 6.25 coins is not expected to be reached until 2020.

Ethereum

Ethereum is a platform rather than a currency, and it is run on the EVM – Ethereum Virtual Machine. The currency produced from Ethereum is called Ether and, rather than being a currency that you can spend or send to another, it is used to fuel the Ethereum platform. The main use for Ethereum is to create and run smart contracts, and these are run on ETH.

These contracts enable the exchange of money, shares, property or anything else that has a value in a way that is free of conflict and transparent, all without the need to employ a middleman to oversee things. In short, a currency or an asset is transferred into the program, which will then run the code. At a certain point, the code will evaluate a specific condition and, if that condition is validated, it will then determine if the asset or currency is to be forwarded to the recipient or returned to the original sender. For example, let's say that I am going to rent you an apartment and we are going to do this by using cryptocurrency on the blockchain. We have a virtual contract, and I will give you a digital entry key by a set date. If I don't send the key on time, a refund is automatically released to you. If the key is sent before the due date, it will be held by the system and, on the date specified in the contract, both the key and the funds will be released to the respective parties. The entire process works on a system that is witnessed by millions of people and should, in theory, run seamlessly and automatically. If I supply the key, I get paid; if you send the currency, you get the key. The contract will have a set cancellation date, which will come into effect on the date specified, and neither party can interfere with the code.

Smart contracts can be used for all sorts of things and are compatible with all wallets and any exchange that uses one of the standard coin APIs. Right now, they have an average block time of about 20 seconds, but their aim is to reach 12 seconds, significantly faster than the Bitcoin block time. There are a number of Ethereum clones out there, and the Ethereum platform is also responsible for hosting several other tokens, such as Augur and DigixDAO, making Ethereum less of a single cryptocurrency and rather more like a family.

Litecoin

Litecoin, or LTC as it is abbreviated to, is a Bitcoin alternative and not a Bitcoin replacement as some think. Where Bitcoin is the gold, Litecoin is the silver, using many of the Bitcoin fundamentals but changing parts of it, so it becomes a viable alternative. Where Bitcoin takes vast amounts of power to mine a block, Litecoin is more suited to those of you that want to mine form your own home computer, without having to spend wads of cash on expensive hardware and, if you get in there early enough, you should be able to use this to your advantage – mine now and hold your winnings until the price goes up.

Litecoin is much faster than Bitcoin, with a block time of around 2.5 minutes and it uses a different mining algorithm. It is also capped at 84 million coins, much more than Bitcoin's 21 million. While it has no real use case, it has facilitated the development and emergence of a number of other crypto coins, such as FeatherCoin and Dogecoin. Litecoin is still developed and traded actively and tends to be hoarded as a serious backup should Bitcoin ever fail.

Ripple

Ripple has its own cryptocurrency coin, the XRP but it is less about that currency and more about being a network that processes IOUs. XRP is not a medium for the storage and exchange of value like the BTC or LTC, for example. Instead, it is a token that is used to provide protection to the network against instances of spam.

Every single XRP token has been created by Ripple Labs, the developers behind the Ripple network and these tokens are distributed at will by Ripple Labs. This earns it the reputation of being a pre-mined currency within the cryptocurrency community and tends to be dismissed as not being real. As such, it doesn't tend to be pushed as a worthwhile investment for a store of value. There are said to be a total of 100 million Ripple tokens planned with just half going into circulation and the rest being held back by the developers.

Ripple has placed itself as a complement to Bitcoin and not a competitor, touting themselves as a way of transferring currency, be it fiat or digital, seamlessly. Not only do they promise to provide Bitcoin users with more connection options in terms of other currencies, but they also promise better stability and faster transactions. Because Ripple is a distributed network, there is no dependence on a single company of the management and security of the blockchain database. That means not having to wait for block confirmations, and any transaction confirmation can be pushed through very quickly.

One major use case for Ripple is the financial institutions; the banks love Ripple and are adopting it in increasingly more cases. They use it as a way of connection banks, corporations, digital asset exchanges and payment providers through RippleNet as a way of providing an easy way to send money anywhere in the world.

OmiseGO

OmiseGO has been built on Ethereum and is positioning itself to be the top-ranked P2P cryptocurrency platform. It isn't just an altcoin; OmiseGO is more of a financial platform and has one purpose in mind – to disrupt the methods that most financial institutions use today. We are talking about the way that we currently buy and sell cryptocurrencies through an exchange and OmiseGO has some pretty forward ideas.

They connect all the cryptocurrency wallets that are currently in existence to on centralized blockchain and, over this blockchain, users can very quickly and easily exchange their currencies. Most of today's exchanges are centralized with data being stored on a central server or server group. OmiseGO doesn't do this – all transactions on the OmiseGO platform are decentralized, stored only on the blockchain. This ensures the security of the data because blockchains can't be hacked very easily. And, in terms of money transfer, exchanges require you to exchange fiat for cryptocurrency and then let you change it back, but they will charge you a fee for each step. For example, if you had BTC and you wanted to buy ETH, you would need to send your BTC to an exchange that offers a trade in both currencies. Next, your BTC would need to be exchanged for fiat currency, and then you can buy the ETH. OmiseGO does away with this unwieldy system by allowing you to do one direct conversion, from BTC straight to ETH, for example, with just one small fee.

This system will allow for much easier transactions, such as making payments, payroll deposits, remittances, supply chain finances, asset management and many other on-demand services in a way that is totally decentralized, highly secure, easy to use and cheaper.

Currently, if you own OMG, the OmiseGO token, it is not possible to exchange it or spend it; it can only be stored in your wallet as an investment. And, the only way to get OMG is to use fiat currency to purchase it through an exchange. OMG tokens are also used as a way of validating transactions on the network; correct validation earns the winner some of the fees from the transaction. This is similar to the method of mining used with Bitcoin with the exception that there is no need for expensive hardware that eats up the electricity costs. By contrast to Bitcoin, if a miner validates a Bitcoin block wrong, it costs them in power; with OMG, the validator loses money in other ways, i.e., a proportion of their OMG token holdings.

CHAPTER FIVE:
CRYPTOCURRENCY REGULATIONS

In the economic market, cryptocurrency has been emerging as an investment asset that's smart, prospective and quite promising. Despite its volatile character and the risks involved, crypto coins have established themselves in the digital market, and traders and investors have been flocking to them. In the world of cryptocurrency, Bitcoin has proved itself not only to be one of the oldest players but also as the most popular, since 2009. Its sensational increase in value has shot up the confidence among investors.

While there still exists some confusion surrounding the purchase of a cryptocurrency; the financial market has been successful in showing an incline in the numbers of people who've bought the coins, invested or profited from trading them with different crypto coins. Profiting from trading different cryptocurrencies, buying or selling them, or even making money by converting assets (wealth) from, say, Bitcoin or other coins to 'fiat money' and vice versa are all possible scenarios. When the regulatory bodies understood that using all this virtual money was resulting in quite a flow of money in vast amounts, they sought to regulate this flow of digital coins; and this was done by virtual money being imposed with taxation.

As per the **Internal Revenues Service (IRS)**, cryptocurrency is being referred to as 'personal property' and not as a currency, and that makes it taxable. To further elaborate – for the traders or investors, generating income from selling cryptocurrencies is being subjected either to long-term or short-term taxations. The ones who'd find the taxation process to be favorable are the retirement account investors. While the tax isn't levied on them, persons interested in 'mining' Bitcoins will be subjected to taxation since mining itself is seen as a business income source.

If an asset (crypto coins) is held on a long-term basis (i.e., exceeding a twelve-month period), and based on the value of the income, the trader or investor will be subjected to 15%-20% income tax rates. On the other hand, when held for a short-term period (less than twelve-months), they'll be subjected to normal income tax rates. Tax value and time period can differ country to country; it can also depend on a nation's tax laws and currency value.

Taxation of Cryptocurrency

Countries looking to place regulations on cryptocurrencies are using either of the following to define them:

- Asset
- Asset Value
- Commodity
- Property

Despite not treating digital currencies like 'technical currencies' they can still be exchanged for fiat currencies like USD, INR, EUR. Moreover, they can be traded with different goods or services, and other cryptocurrencies. The regulators are seeking to snatch control and track monetary flows taking place between traders and investors – to oversee all the transactions in a more detailed manner, which is why they're forcing regulations on digital currencies. Anyone partaking in cryptocurrency transactions will be subjected to income tax or general tax based on their nationality's tax policies. In most countries, tax regulators have been defining cryptocurrencies as income made through cryptocurrency trading (mostly, Bitcoin trading), or as a 'property' acquired from capital investments.

Different Countries and Regulation Perspectives

- **Japan**: Bitcoin is viewed at with the value of something asset-like. It's recognized as an official 'mode of payment.' Selling Bitcoins has been exempted from consumption law, as of 1st July 2017. However, gaining profits from crypto trading (i.e., Bitcoin) means paying company tax, capital gains tax, or income tax depending on the rate of income.
- **Australia:** Have exempted cryptocurrencies from GST (Goods-and-Services Tax).
- **European Union (EU):** Has termed cryptocurrency as foreign currency.
- **Germany:** Considers 'mining' to be a business. And mining cryptocurrency will subject the person to

paying 'company tax.' Holding Bitcoins for a period exceeding twelve months won't subject them to being taxed on capital gains.

- **UK, Switzerland, and Germany:** Cryptocurrency transactions have been exempted from VAT fees.

In countries like Brazil, Canada, US, UK, Germany, and Australia, if taxpayers hold on to the investments they've made in cryptocurrency, they'll be subjected to a range of anywhere from 0% to 25% of capital gains tax.

Most of the countries view profits acquired from cryptocurrency trading as a 'business income' source, which, by default, makes them applicable for paying company tax, income tax, or capital tax depending on the rate of income.

Factors leading up to the Taxation of Cryptocurrencies

- 'Like-kind' is the tax code exemption being quoted by most cryptocurrency investors to avoid paying any kind of taxes on crypto exchanges.

- Crypto traders used to use properties (real estate) and creative articles (arts) as a means of exchange without paying any transactional taxes since cryptocurrency had not been declared to be 'taxable property.'

- Traders benefitted a lot from transactions taking place under the 'like-kind' tax code; they made huge profits without paying taxes for cryptocurrency exchanges. This led to the IRS releasing a statement that cryptocurrency will now be considered a 'property' and no longer a currency.

- Lawyers and financial advisors alike have made interpretations of one cryptocurrency being exchanged with another without a need to pay transactional taxes because as the 'like-kind' code implies – 'properties' can be exchanged or traded with tax exemptions.

- As per the IRS, during the transaction of 'attainment of capital or monetary gain,' when cryptocurrency investors exchanged two crypto coins (one with another), they were taxed on capital gains.

A cryptocurrency exchange, Coinbase, quite popular too, faced strict measures to hand in records of their investors from the year 2013 to 2015 when crypto investors failed at filing their tax returns and couldn't publish the profits and losses made via cryptocurrency investments for the said years. Once this chapter was done, regulations were made for all the cryptocurrency transactions, steps taken, and the virtual currency was put under immense scrutiny.

As cryptocurrency's value keeps indicating a constant increase with each passing day, investors and traders with the majority of their investments being in the cryptocurrency domain would have to pay capital gain taxes, income taxes, high transaction fees, etc. Vast amounts of resources are being spent on technology to keep track of all the Bitcoin and cryptocurrency users. However, if anything, the world of cryptocurrencies might counteract that with technology that is much more complicated. That is – 'cryptography.'

Bitcoins and Tax

Bitcoin traders and investors will be subjected to taxation based on the frequency of their transaction.

Let's have a look at how Bitcoin transactions, as an 'income' mode, would be treated:

- Gains are emerging from Bitcoins as a result of trading: Business income.
- Buying and selling Bitcoins regularly where gains are business income, and loss equals to business loss: Business income and business loss.
- Prices are increasing when Bitcoins are held as an investment, followed by a trade: Source income.
- When bought only as an investment: Capital assets.

For profits made by selling Bitcoins, which are held for longer durations, it is capital gains tax that the investor will have to pay. Capital gains of the short-term nature, that is, Bitcoins being held for a duration of less than thirty-six months, are taxable depending on the tax regulations of the investor's country. As for the long-term gains, Bitcoins held for a period of more than thirty-six months, and these would be taxed at 20% income value, at the maximum.

Chapter Six: Your Mindset

The investor's mindset plays a vital role. Here are a few short tips to help you with structuring a mindset that would benefit you as a cryptocurrency investor:

- Look at your investments as an endeavor that's long term.
- Be positive in a genuine and realistic way.
- Know that sometimes you win; sometimes you lose.
- Be sure to question everything. Research, research, research!
- Good profits even come in the form of small profits.
- Patience and persistence always pay off.
- Stay away from the media and its 'experts.'
- Don't sell it all when the market is piping hot.
- Diversifying for the sake of diversifying is a no.
- Learn to cut down your losses.
- Form a thick skin.

These are just some hot mantras that you need to keep in mind when dealing with any cryptocurrency. Don't forget to research well before getting on the cryptocurrency bandwagon.

Conclusion

The cryptocurrency market is a fast one with wild volatility. Every day, we see new ones, we see old ones disappear, and we see people making serious money or losing it fast. Each new cryptocurrency comes with its own set of promises, mostly a promise that they are going to turn the world on its head. Few make it past the first couple of months, many get pumped and then dumped by early speculators, leaving them hanging on as a zombie coin until it is clear there is no money to be made.

However, the future of the cryptocurrency is such that, in years to come, they will be seen as legitimate forms some business transactions, remittances, and micropayments. The money will be moved instantly, with little to no fees attached and others will use the technology for creating smart contracts and to revolutionize the entire business world.

Like it or not, cryptocurrencies are real, and they are here to stay. They will change the way we do business, the way we see money, and this is already starting to happen. People purchase cryptocurrencies as a hedge against their own national currency being devalued. More and more businesses are using smart contracts; even governments and central banks are getting in on the act. You have two choices – stand by and watch or join the revolution.

Was this book helpful? Could you please leave an honest review at:

https://www.amazon.com/dp/B077PG7BBX

Thank you!

www.ingramcontent.com/pod-product-compliance
Lightning Source LLC
Chambersburg PA
CBHW030059230526
45471CB00003B/1165